T0160702

'da Kink in my hair

'da Kink in my hair

trey anthony

Playwrights Canada Press
Toronto • Canada

LIBRARY AND ARCHIVES CANADA CATALOGUING IN PUBLICATION
anthony, trey
    'da kink in my hair / trey anthony.

A play.
ISBN 978-0-88754-756-0

1. Women, Black--West Indies--Drama. I. Title. II. Title: Kink in my hair.

PS8601.N73D3 2005   C813'.6   C2005-900232-8

Playwrights Canada Press acknowledges that we operate on land which, for thousands of years, has been the traditional territories of the Mississaugas of the New Credit, the Huron-Wendat, the Anishinaabe, Métis, and the Haudenosaunee peoples. Today, this meeting place is still home to many Indigenous people from across Turtle Island and we are grateful to have the opportunity to work and play here.

We acknowledge the financial support of the Canada Council for the Arts—which last year invested $153 million to bring the arts to Canadians throughout the country—the Ontario Arts Council (OAC), Ontario Creates, and the Government of Canada for our publishing activities.

 Canada Council Conseil des arts
for the Arts   du Canada

ONTARIO ARTS COUNCIL
CONSEIL DES ARTS DE L'ONTARIO
an Ontario government agency
un organisme du gouvernement de l'Ontario

 Canadä

ONTARIO CREATES | ONTARIO CRÉATIF

Dedication

'da Kink is dedicated to beautiful janet...
for allowing me to always remain rooted in my truth.
Loving fiercely without conditions.

Also to my mother, grandmother, Reneé and Darren and
Dad.

And to every little Black girl who has ever dreamed bigger
than her circumstances.

Acknowledgements

To janet for proof-reading, inspiration, belief and love.

My family for always giving me something to write about....

Dee and V, Jean and Rachael for true friendship and helping me deal with the shit, when it is too difficult to write it down.

Thank you to Weyni Mengesha for directing the play, and bringing words from paper to life. You are an extremely talented womyn!

A special thanks to the Kink family for being patient with the process. For believing in the work when all we had was hope.

Djanet Sears for being an inspiration and role model.

To all the community radio stations, colleges, universities and media who have supported my work.

Much love to Layne Coleman and all the staff at Theatre Passe Muraille for showing us what the show could be with a budget.

Angela Rebeiro for publishing the play and being extremely patient with me.

Contents

Foreword

'da Kink in my hair is a remarkable illustration of story as a nutri-
tion for the soul. This first major play by trey anthony shows her
to be one of the most gifted and vibrant writers for the stage to
come along in many years. Ingeniously, trey has not only created
an incredible ensemble Black women's voices, but her powerful
use of the personal narrative stylistically links her work to an
African oral tradition that has survived and still thrives in the
African Diaspora in spite of a separation of four centuries and
a vast ocean. Moreover, her choice to set the entire piece in a
Caribbean Canadian hairdressing salon has enormous resonance
for Black women. For no other racial or cultural group is a hair
style also a personal and political statement which reflects the
beliefs, the history, the aspirations, the pain, the jubilation and the
contradictions of many Black women's lives.

The business of Black hair is almost a $500-million-dollar industry
in the United States. Here in Toronto, all one has to do is pick up
a Share Magazine, a Pride Newspaper or one of any number of
African Canadian or Caribbean Canadian weeklies to see that the
overwhelming number of advertisements in these publications
come from hairdressing salons and barbers to deduce that a rela-
tively similar proportion of Black Torontonians spend their hard
earned dollars in the same fashion. Still, what this phenomenon
does not entirely reveal is the significance of Black hair salons to
Black women on a psychological level.

Many of us growing up Black and female can relate harrowing
tales of being told we have either "bad hair" (read more African),
or "good hair" (read more European). To straighten or to 'fro?
That is most often the question. One choice sometimes connot-
ing an aspiration towards European values of beauty, the other
possibly either a reaction against it, or an embracing of ones own
African-ness. This ultimately raises the questions, when is a hair
style just a hair style? or is a hair style really always a statement?
In attempting to untangle the roots of our obsession with hair,
one might begin to see hair as a metaphor for not only our history, but for our present-day psyches. This is what makes a Black
hairdressing salon more than a beautician's parlour. For while

a Black hairstylist might be able to do everything from shape and trim your 'fro, braid (with or without extensions), cornrow, corkscrew, press (with a hot comb) and/or chemically straighten your tightly coiled tresses. For a majority of women in the Black community, the hairdresser is the closest thing to a head doctor we ever (voluntarily) encounter. She/he will not only twist your dreadlocks, weave very expensive Korean women's hair into your head, colour your jet black, off-black, dark brown, auburn, copper, tawny or Beyonce blond hair, but she/he will also listen, with the attention of a first-rate therapist, to your countless joys and all of your woes. Now the fact that everyone else in the salon can hear every sordid detail of your story is not usually a call to silence, for all have come to see the head doctor and they too shall soon have their turn to work through the kinks.

This is what anthony achieves with the play. She gives voice to the "kink", the coil, the loop, the twist, the flaw, the painful contraction, the frizz, the sharp bend produced when a loop in a line is pulled way too tight, the fit of laughter (for 'da KinK in my hair is as incredibly funny, as it is moving). In presenting a hairdressing salon as a place of transformation, 'da KinK in my hair requires that we let the stories wash over us; detangling the knots of denial and confusion; locking the multiple curls and twists of our identities in an act of self acceptance.

In the same way that we never leave a hair stylist's lair the same way we enter it, the characters in this breathtaking story are not merely attempting to get things straight within themselves, they are, in the words sentiment of the great Marcus Garvey, not endeavouring to remove the kinks from their hair; they are attempting to remove the kinks from their minds.

Djanet Sears

Playwright/Adjunct Professor
University College, University of Toronto

December, 2004

The history of 'da Kink

'da Kink in my hair was originally conceptualised as a one womyn show. Playwright and comedian trey anthony had just recently ended a seven-year relationship, and turned to her computer for consolation. She wanted to write a play that would focus on the lives of black womyn and authentically reflect the joy, hardship, and struggles of a Black womyn's lives. She wanted to incorporate her own personal story and also stories and "gossip" that she heard to make *'da Kink* believable. Seven months later the first rough draft of *'da Kink* was born.

trey invited six of her "closest friends," (who just happen to be the best female actors in Toronto) over for an informal reading and to get feedback about the pieces that she had written. The feedback was amazing! Her friends convinced trey that the monologues needed to be heard. trey had a feeling that she might be on to something but still was a bit skeptical. She decided to hold a public reading of *'da Kink* in a small downtown coffee lounge and send out a public invite via email. She wanted to hear what the monologues would sound like aloud and get some objective feedback. The reading was a sold-out hit, and trey extended it for one more night which also immediately sold-out!

trey gave out audience surveys and the response was very positive. People really loved the pieces but some people commented that the pieces were very dark, emotional, and heavy. trey went back to her computer to think how was it possible to add humour to such serious topics as incest, homophobia, police brutality, etc. That's when her comedic experience "kicked in" and trey developed the comedic outrageous character, Novelette, who would bring all the serious pieces together, yet add humor to the play. trey immediately abandoned the idea of making *'da Kink* a one womyn's show and invited her friends along for a kinky journey. *'da Kink in my hair* had been reborn...

'da Kink in my hair made it's first full-length dramatic debut at the Toronto Fringe Festival in July 2001. The play was produced by Plaitform Entertainment which was trey's production and entertainment company. The "buzz" was already on the street that this

was the show to see! The show sold-out every night, with people lining up for hours ahead of the show to get tickets! Disappointed people were turned away nightly! The show was hailed by the *Toronto Sun* as the "Pick of the fringe!" The show also received a Critic's pick by *Now Magazine* and was also selected as best cast ensemble. The show also boasted the highest ticket sales of all the shows in the Toronto Fringe Festival!

Due to the success of the Fringe, trey was asked by the Harbourfront Centre to remount the show again for its Black History, Kuumba Festival. All four shows sold out weeks ahead of the scheduled performances and the show received standing ovations every night.

In June of 2003 *'da Kink* was remounted at Theatre Passe Muraille. Again the show was a sold-out success, receiving standing ovations every night. The play received the highest box office sales in Theatre Passe Muraille's history!

'da Kink was selected by Mirvish Productions, Canada's largest independent theatre producer of plays such as *The Lion King*, *Hairspray* and *Mamma Mia!*, for a six-week week run which began in January 2005, and which was extended several times, eventually closing at the end of April 2005. It was also the first Canadian play to be produced at the Princess of Wales Theatre.

Playwright's Notes

When I dare to be powerful, to use my strength in the service of my vision, then it becomes less and less important whether I am afraid.   – Audre Lorde, *Sister Outsider*

Writing '*da Kink in my hair*, saved my life. Each one of the characters has some small part of me and my life embedded in their Voice. They became my Voice when I was too afraid too speak, too afraid to act, too afraid to question, too afraid to be loved, give love or demand to be treated gently, kindly, and with respect. The first draft of '*da Kink* was written four years ago, and I am thankful that I am now at a different place in my life. Yet these womyn's Voices are always present within me. I have sat, dined, cried and laughed with these characters for many years. My writing has been my peace of mind, my own act of defiance to change the world in some small but significant way. I am braver in my writing; I am bold. Fierce. Demanding. Uncompromising. Uncensored. Writing allows me for a minute to stop the fears that continue to plague me in my daily life. The constant fears of not being good enough, worth enough, deserving enough.... Before writing '*da Kink* I used to live with my fears in solitude and I now realise that many people live their lives in a constant state of fear. That fear is usually fed, nurtured, expected and accepted. Usually when one tries to arise from fear, to be bold, honest, truer to self, many will discourage that. For myself it is a constant battle to live my life without fear and to be less afraid. There are times that my fear paralyses and silences me. Times when I look fear in the eye and laugh until my stomach aches. Times that I have hidden myself, feelings and thoughts because it is easier. Times that I have lied to myself and others because the truth would be much more difficult. Times when I cry until I am sure there could not possibly be any tears left. Yet there are many times when I am bold and truthful. And I know I have no other choice but to continue and trust that I must do this... Continue to write, question, and speak loudly. Be able to live my life with truth, honesty and without fear. I used to think that somehow I would reach a final fearless and peaceful destination and I could remain there. Somehow I would eventually be at a place and know this is "It". I

am finally here! Yet I now realise this is a continued journey and everyday I am challenged to try and be the best person that I can be. I must remain committed to being less afraid. Committed to standing in my truth. Be committed to be rooted in my truth.
Blessings
trey

'da Kink in my hair was first produced by Plaitform Entertainment in association with Theatre Passe Muraille June 2003:

trey anthony	NOVELETTE
Zena Brown	LADY ONE
Raven Dauda	SHARMAINE
Miranda Edwards	SHERELLE
Quancetia Hamilton	SHAWNETTE
Ngozi Paul	NIA
Ordena Stephens	PATSY
d'bi.young	STACEY-ANNE

Percussion/Vocals by Amina Alfred

dub poem uncle john written by d'bi.young

Directed by Weyni Mengesha
Set Design & Props by janet romero
Lighting Design by Rebecca Picharack
Costume Design by Caffery VanHorn
Musical Directions & Arrangement by Alejandra Nunez
Movement Design by Ma'at Zachary & Roger C. Jeffrey
Movement Transition & Music Written by Weyni Mengesha
Stage Managed by Trina Sookhai

'da kink in my hair was presented by Mirvish Productions at The Princess of Wales Theatre, January 11 to February 27, 2005 and extended four times until it eventually closed on April 24, 2005.

Amina Alfred	Vocalist / Percussionist
trey anthony	Novelette
Jully Black	Vocalist
Zena Brown	Milly
Guiomar Campbell	Percussionist
Lisa Codrington	Maxine
Raven Dauda	Sharmaine
Miranda Edwards	Sherelle
Quancetia Hamilton	Shawnette
Abena Malika	Reign
Weyni Mengesha	Percussionist
Alejandra Nunez	Percussionist
Ngozi Paul	Nia
Rachael-Lea Rickards	Diana
Satori Shakoor	Miss Enid
Ordena Stephens-Thompson	Patsy
d'bi.young	Stacey-Anne

Directed by Weyni Mengesha

Set & Costume Design	Julia Tribe
Lighting Design	Rebecca Picharack
Musical Directions & Arrangement	Alejandra Nunez
Choreographer	Fleurette S. Fernando
Music & Lyrics	Weyni Mengesha
Assistant Choreographer	Ma'at Zachary
Technical Producer	John Wilbur
Associate Producer	Linda Intaschi
Additional Casting	Dayton Walters Casting
Assistant Director	Dian Marie Bridge
Stage Manager	Michael Sinclair
Assistant Stage Manager	Trina Sookhai

Dub Poem "in honour of belief" by d'bi.young

Act One

Opening Scene

Stage dimly lit, a hairdressing shop. Alone on the stage is a hairdressing chair, at the edge of the stage is a tight coil, representing the hair. The Griot enters, she then calls the Goddess who enters proudly she blesses the stage. The Griot then calls the dancers/community who enter. They dance, this is a celebratory dance. Suddenly there is an urgent beat on the drum and the dancers stop. They reach for the coil which is sitting at the edge of the stage, which is abruptly pulled apart, and a frightful sound escape occurs as the dancers stop and they reenact the sizzling, frying, pain, agony and torture that black hair is subjected too. The drums beat faster and angry. It becomes a desperate frenzy of cries and moans and then there is a final beat of the drum and women take the afro pics and place them on the edge of the stage. Black out.

NOVELETTE enters.

Salon: Lights up on NOVELETTE, who sits in the hairdressing chair putting on her makeup. All the other women are frozen in tableau.

NOVELETTE
(*addresses the audience*) My work is never done! I'm always working, working, working. You want me to talk to you, explain what's going on in this play well forget it! Pick up a program and read it or something because I have no time to talk to you today! I'm a busy busy career woman. No time for myself. Isn't that true Miss Lizzy. (*She addresses the plant.*) Oh I need to water you. Can't forget about you. Don't worry Miss Lizzy. I'll get you your water soon. I have so much things to do... It never stops. (*She grabs the broom and begins sweeping.*) I'm telling you between doing my makeup, sweeping, and of course doing hair, the work never stops! Being a hair-dresser is not an easy thing. (*She walks over to the women frozen in tableau.*) people rushing in here talking about oh Novelette, I want this style, this cut, this washed, this coloured, don't they see I'm busy—

MILLY bursts through tableau and proceeds towards NOVELETTE.

MILLY

Excuse me, pardon me.

The other women come out of tableau and the store becomes alive. A busy hustle and bustle. The women become the customers and it is business as usual at NOVELETTE's hair salon. Three women take their places at their seats chatting. CLAUDETTE and SANDRA are gossiping at the cash register. DIANA is doing MARCIA's nails at the nail booth.

Excuse me! I have a seven-thirty appointment and it's now eleven-thirty and you haven't started my hair yet.

NOVELETTE

(*She looks MILLY up and down with distaste.*) See what I mean. Listen here lady. I said come for seven-thirty I did not state anywhere or at any time I would start you at seven-thirty because, you booked an appointment you never book a guarantee. Now sit down and when I'm ready for you I'll let you know!

MILLY sheepishly returns to seat. NOVELETTE addresses the audience again.

Out of order! I'm telling you if it's not one thing it's the other. women rushing in here, looking like they got run over by a Mac truck, then expecting me to make them look like Janet Jackson. I said lady I'm a hairdresser not a magician! And I tell you as a hairdresser you get to know everybody's business.

DIANA

Did I tell your I saw your boyfriend in the mall with his sister.

REIGN

What sister? Derrick doesn't have a sister!

DIANA

Then who is she then?

DIANA gives a knowing smile to the other ladies in the shop, who laugh nervously.

NOVELETTE

I'm telling you, I get to know everybody's business! Not
that I'm a nosy or anything. But if they don't tell you
the hair will. Don't believe me? Well let me tell you…
my mother was a hairdresser, my mother's mother was
a hairdresser, and my granny granny, (*She counts on her
fingers.*) granny, granny use to be a hairdresser. I'm telling
you, it's been a long time since us Campbells have been
doing hair. We are very entrepreneurish. And my granny
granny, granny, granny, granny, granny, granny, used to
s… If you want to know about a woman, a black woman
that is. Touch her hair. Cause our hair carries our journey. 'Cause that's where we carry all our hopes, all our
dreams, our hurt, our disappointments they're all in our
hair.

CLAUDETTE

Yeah gal, me and Jean Paul pun di speaker box!

> *She gives an elaborate sexual dance move, the other
> women cheer.*

NOVELETTE

(*She shakes her head.*) Why do you think it's kinky? We
got all our sexual fantasies in there too! (*She laughs.*) You
don't believe me well watch this! Come I'm ready for
you. (*She walks over to CLAUDETTE and SANDRA and
interrupts their conversation.*) Claudette, you're my favourite niece but I will not hesitate to fire you. Again! Would
you like to do some work around here today please!

> *She hands CLAUDETTE the broom and looks disap-
> provingly at SANDRA.*

SANDRA

I'll call you. (*NOVELETTE looks at her.*) Later?

> *SANDRA gives a quick wave and exits the salon.
> MILLY enters the chair and begins flipping through a
> magazine. NOVELETTE starts to touch her hair. As
> her fingers are going through the hair the hair sends
> her a message. NOVELETTE knows exactly what's
> going on. NOVELETTE closes her eyes her fingers
> entwined deeply in the woman's hair. She inhales and
> laughs softly to herself as she addresses the audience.*

NOVELETTE
> Pay attention. Watch this. She's cheating on her husband. He's lousy in bed. Viagra didn't help him. And not only is she cheating. She's cheating with her best friend's husband. Dirty little hussy!

MILLY
> (*looks up startled*) Excuse me?

NOVELETTE
> (*quickly*) I said I hope you're not too fussy.

MILLY
> Well could you hurry up I got things to see and people to do. I mean people to see.

NOVELETTE
> I'm sure you do. Well Claudette will finish you off. (*She yells for CLAUDETTE.*) Claudette!

CLAUDETTE
> I'm coming! Auntie Letty, you think I can get next week Friday off?

NOVELETTE
> Sure you can, Friday, Saturday, whatever. Take as much time as you think you need. Claudette, as a matter of fact don't even come back! Now finish Milly off and give her a b twelve Kerasilk rinse deep conditioning. Understand? Good girl.

> MILLY *exits the stage with a sullen looking CLAUDETTE. NOVELETTE walks to the edge of the stage and addresses the audience.*

NOVELETTE
> I'm telling you the hair sends me a message. Some of the things it tells me makes me want to laugh, makes me want to cry. And some of the things it tells me I don't even want to know. Because some of us are hurting. Hurting real bad. And you know as women we cry, cry a lot. Cry on the inside too proud to cry on the outside. And some of the things, which the hair tells me, makes

me, want to cry. But I don't I keep it up here. (*touches her head*) Right here in my head. Right here in my hair. The things I hear is right here in my hair! Anyways I'll talk to you!

> *NOVELETTE walks back to her chair and indicates for DIANE to enter it. NOVELETTE begins pulling the rollers out of DIANE's hair and starts to style it as the other women chatter grows. TRINA yells from across the room to NOVELETTE.*

TRINA

Novelette, isn't it true that Revlon paid her four million dollars to dye her hair blonde and now she's their spokes-model.

REIGN

A Black woman with blonde hair that's not right. Why does a sista think she needs to do that?

MARCIA

Four million dollars hello!

REIGN

So she couldn't keep her black hair and still be in their ad?

DIANA

Well, I think she looks absolutely fabulous! Not everybody has the colouring to wear blonde.

NOVELETTE

Well not every fashion fits everybody and—

MARCIA

Well for four million dollars I would dye my hair blonde.

TRINA

Dirty blonde!

MARCIA

Honey blonde!

TRINA

Corn field, barley growing blonde!

MARCIA
Even a black natural blonde for four million dollars!

All the women laugh.

REIGN
Letty I know you wouldn't do it.

DIANA
Wait you haven't seen her in her blonde wig?

MARCIA
Letty's dangerous!

TRINA
Fierce!

MARCIA
Watch out little Kim!

NOVELETTE
Ok, you two enough. Don't start with me and my wig. Me, I just do whatever makes me happy. Come Shawney I ready for you.

> *SHAWNEY makes her way over to the chair and sits down.*

But Shawney, I haven't seen you in awhile. But what happen to your locks? They need twisting.

SHAWNETTE
I know...

NOVELETTE
Your hair is a mess. What is going on? Didn't I show you how to twist them yourself?

SHAWNETTE
Yes and I—

NOVELETTE
Shawney, this hair has not been twisted the roots are showing.

SHAWNETTE
I know. But I've been so busy.

NOVELETTE looks at her with concern.

NOVELETTE
To busy too have time for yourself?

(*touching her hair with concern*) No time? Shawney, it's ok sometimes to put yourself first.

> *NOVELETTE places her fingers deep into SHAWNETTE's hair. As her fingers reach into SHAWNETTE's hair the GRIOTS sing a soft melody and there is a lighting transition. SHAWNETTE gets up from the chair and walks to the centre spotlight.*

SHAWNETTE
I got a kink in my hair.

CHORUS
Kink. Kink in my hair.

SHAWNETTE
You use to love to play with that kink in my hair when it was all sweaty and damp. Kinky hair matted to my face. Sweat and your love dripping between my thighs. My love and me imprinted on your ebony skin. And you tracing my nose with your tongue. You just loving the roundness of my butt, grabbing chocolate brown skin between your fingers. Kneading me like dough. Kneading chocolate dough.

CHORUS & SHAWNETTE
(*beat*) Needing me?

SHAWNETTE
And we sat in that match-box apartment dreaming about the house on the hills, the Benz in the driveway, the maid getting the door, our kids running around. I said my girl would have a pony and you said my little man gonna take golf lessons or something. (*laughs softly*) And let me tell you I would go to the beauty parlour all day. Get my nails done and do my hair. And you would say baby, do those nails and even them bad feet, but don't get rid of that kink in your hair.

CHORUS
Kink in your hair. Kink in my hair.

SHAWNETTE
And back then times were rough. Real rough! A can of tuna was an appetizer, a three course meal and a late night snack. And you use to say "Baby, pretend it's caviar." And I tasted the caviar. Tasted your hunger. Tasted your thirst. Tasted your need to fill me up. And I became full. Full on your hopes, dreams, full with your desires. (*beat*) Satisfied with just you I became full.

CHORUS
Full. I'm full.

SHAWNETTE
Unbuckled my belt buckle as my stomach overflowed with you and your wishful food of dreams. And we laughed and we dreamed. And we dreamed and we laughed. And you played with that kink in my hair.

CHORUS
Kink in my hair. Kink.

SHAWNETTE
We had a plan. I got another job so you could go to med school. (*beat*) Left you studying at night as I caught the five Downtown train of Faith, connecting to the number 23 bus of Hope. I cleaned those offices and I dreamed.

CHORUS
Dreamed.

SHAWNETTE
I ate caviar sandwiches on my ten-minute break. And when I came home all tired and torn you played with that kink in my hair.

CHORUS
Kink in my hair. Kink.

SHAWNETTE
Sweat and your love dripping between my thighs. (*beat*) Filling me up again with you!

CHORUS
You? You. You!

SHAWNETTE

You! So forgive me if I feel to choke now! I got a burning desire to spit you the fuck out! (*beat*) Because I paid my dues!

CHORUS & SHAWNETTE

I did my time! I made you! I loved you! I believed you! I still love you. (*softer tone and in disbelief*)

SHAWNETTE

So I just don't get when it became so important to you that I didn't have a college education. Every time we got invited to a colleague's dinner party, you held your breath every time I spoke. Heard lies coming out of your mouth as you invented who I needed to be, who you thought I should be. All the education I got, and all the degrees I never earned. (*beat*) But you forgot to tell them that my education was about love, trust, and honesty! It was about us! Me loving you and you loving me.

CHORUS

You loving me. Me?

Two beats.

SHAWNETTE

Yet all too soon, the kink in my hair.

CHORUS

Kink. Kink in my hair.

SHAWNETTE

Me? I just couldn't seem to fit into your dreams. You trying desperately to change me. But I had to resist when you tried to erase me…

CHORUS

Erase? Erase me.

SHAWNETTE

(*two beats*) So now I'm here and she's there. She's in our home. She's in our bed. Lying in my sweat and my tears. She's the mother of your children. (*beat*) How come she's got my life? I don't think she remembers tuna caviar! (*beat*) I don't think she mended your spirit and patched up your soul! (*beat*) She met you! But she never dreamed you! Believed you! She could never dream you…

CHORUS
>Dream? Dream you. Dream.

SHAWNETTE
>She could never dream you. And I know there ain't no kink to play with in her hair. (*beat*) You use to love to play with that kink in my hair.

>*The griots sing a soft melody. Go to black. The lights transition as SHAWNETTE returns to chair. The lights go up with NOVELETTE's fingers still in SHAWNETTE's hair.*

NOVELETTE
>So there you go Shawney. Twisted so nice you can feel the breeze through your locks now. A fresh breeze is good. It helps you think. Makes you see things clearer.

SHAWNETTE
>Thanks Novelette.

>*SHAWNETTE gets up and NOVELETTE walks her over to the cash register.*

NOVELETTE
>And don't you dare come back in here again looking like Donald Trump!

REIGN
>How come no one not offering him four million dollars to change his hair! Question it Sista!

>*SHARMAINE bursts through the door.*

EVERYONE
>Sharmaine!

NOVELETTE
>What are you doing here!

SHARMAINE
>Took the red eye last night. We're filming in Toronto. So I had to come by.

MARCIA
>Oh it's so good to see you. (*She gets up and hugs her.*) We saw you on the Emmys.

TRINA

Letty closed the shop early and we all watched it here.

NOVELETTE

I'm so proud of you. Getting an Emmy. But you know should have had me flown down to Hollywood to do your hair. I could have done it better than them fancy hairdressers you have.

SHARMAINE

I know.

SHAWNETTE

It's great seeing you, (*She hugs her.*) I'm so proud of you. I'm late for work and I better get going. Call me.

SHARMAINE

I will.

MILLY

(*from under the dryer*) Oh my God! I can't believe this! It's you. Stormy Ryan!

SHARMAINE

My real name Sharmaine, Stormy's my television nam—

MILLY

Stormy can I get your autograph? I watch you every day! Young and the heartless is my favourite show! Did you know your husband David didn't really die in the plane crash!

DIANA

I believe it's that dirty Victor Castlemore is keeping him hostage! So Sharmaine don't marry Blair because David is coming back and you don't want to be an adulteress or a floozy. And you know you're the only Black girl on the show and your mother raised you better!

SHARMAINE

Thanks I'll check it all out. Once I get back… on TV… Here you go. (*She signs her autograph.*) So girls what have I missed? It's good to be home. Diana can I get a fill?

DIANA

Of course darling! You know, it's very important to have long flowing red fingernails because red is passion! And you need so much passion when you are doing those love scenes with Blair Philips. Right Letty?

NOVELETTE
You're right, Diana. He's so rugged and handsome. Sometimes I have to turn off the TV and have a quiet moment with myself. If you know what I mean?

DIANA
Letty! I know what you mean.

CLAUDETTE
He's so cute. Him kiss good Sharmaine.

TRINA
It looks pretty good on TV.

MARCIA
Sharmaine! Give us the details! What's he like?

REIGN
I read in *Ebony* that you two are dating.

SHARMAINE
Don't believe everything that you read. But he's nice. However, I'm not dating him.

> *REIGN, MARCIA and TRINA get up and gather excitedly around sharmaine all eager to get the scoop.*

TRINA
So what's the scoop? Who you dating? Some big Hollywood star.

REIGN
Women we must respect Sharmaine's privacy. However, we do require details!

MARCIA
Break it down! Who is he?

CLAUDETTE
When we a go meet him!

MARCIA
You got to bring him to my party next Saturday.

SHARMAINE
Yeah but—

EVERYONE
Bring him!

SHARMAINE
Guys!

DIANA
He must be cute. Sharmaine has good taste, a woman with class, pedigree, intelligence must place herself with the right people. One who lays with dogs rise with fleas.

> *She turns up her nose at CLAUDETTE and it is obvious to everyone that DIANA is referring to CLAUDETTE.*

SHARMAINE
Enough about me! Novelette, who's that guy that you set Miss Thang up with!

NOVELETTE
Trevor!

MARCIA
No Novelette, you set me up with Trevor and he was ugly. Thanks but no thanks. No more love connections stick to hairdressing ok?

NOVELETTE
Well what about Courtney?

TRINA
Uglier than Trevor.

NOVELETTE
Even in the dark?

MARCIA
Especially in the dark!

> *They all start to laugh.*

So Sharmaine, don't try to change the subject. I'm on to you because we can't all help but notice that new hop in your skip.

REIGN
>That new glow on your skin.

DIANA
>That new wiggle in your hips.

NOVELETTE
>Ladies leave her alone!

TRINA
>And you haven't stop smiling since you got in here.

CLAUDETTE
>She's getting something good!

TRINA
>Real good!

REIGN
>So good that she doesn't even want to talk about it! It's that good.

MARCIA
>Did your man turn you out girl!

>>*MARCIA performs a very sexual provocative dance while TRINA cheers her on. NOVELETTE and DIANA are not impressed.*

>Did he having you saying what is my name Miss Hollywood? Come on Miss Hollywood! Did he have you saying oh, baby baby, please—

>>*TRINA joins in and begins to fake an orgasm.*

TRINA
>Oh baby oh oh—(*She screams.*) Oh!!

>>*TRINA drops dramatically to the floor. PATSY walks in during the middle of all of this. EVERYONE notices that PATSY has walked in, except for TRINA. PATSY looks at her with a look of shock on her face.*

PATSY
>Sister Trina, get up off the ground!

TRINA

Oh, sister Patsy. Um um I was just on my way too, um um—

PATSY

We missed you this week at bible study. However, you have already seem to have found the holy ghost. Hallelujah.

> *She dismisses her with a look of distaste, TRINA sheepishly exits the store. PATSY curtly addresses MARCIA.*

MARCIA

Afternoon. Sister Patsy.

PATSY

Marcia, good to see you making constructive use of your time. The devil does create work for idle hands. Amen.

> *NOVELETTE watches this all with amusement and yells over to PATSY.*

NOVELETTE

Lord, Patsy, I didn't think you were coming again. What time you running on West Indian or Christian time?

> *PATSY shakes her head obviously amused.*
> *NOVELETTE quickly ushers PATSY into the chair.*

PATSY

Oh sorry, Letty, prayer meeting ran over. And you know you cannot rush the Lord.

NOVELETTE

(*She laughs gently.*) Well I am glad you made it. You know I've been meaning to come over and have a little tea or a strong drink of rum with you.

PATSY

Oh no, Novelette, you know I am a Christian woman.

NOVELETTE

Well, drink some rum on a Saturday and go to church, drunk on Sunday, God can't be mad at that.

PATSY

Oh the Lord knows I'm going to pray for you darling.

NOVELETTE
> Well while you're praying. You think you could you ask the man up above about the Lottario numbers for me! Because I want to win some money! But Patsy I'm glad you come this week because girl do I have the style for you girl. Claudette where's the magazine that I had for Patsy?

> *She runs behind the counter and rummages through a pile of magazines. CLAUDETTE comes in and matter-of-factly hands her the magazine she is looking for. NOVELETTE grabs it and quickly runs back to the chair and hands the magazine to PATSY.*

NOVELETTE
> Bam!

> *A startled PATSY jumps out of her chair everyone looks over in curiosity.*

NOVELETTE
> (*excited*) Is this you or is this not you!

> *PATSY looks at the magazine disapprovingly.*

PATSY
> This… is definitely not me. No no, Novelette, I'll just have the same style that I get every week. A nice wash and set thanks.

NOVELETTE
> Oh come on Patsy, everybody needs a little change.

DIANA
> Change is good Patsy, Novelette is right.

PATSY
> No, No, I believe if it's not broken don't fix it.

NOVELETTE
> Patsy, I wouldn't say it's not broken! Come man! Come. Time for a change. Hey Claudette don't you think it's time Patsy change her look.

> *CLAUDETTE walks from behind the counter and whispers loudly in PATSY's ear in order to prove her point.*

CLAUDETTE
A time, Pasty. A time!

PATSY
(*gives CLAUDETTE a bad look but takes another look at the magazine*) You know, I don't think it will suit me. It will make me look too um um… young and party going and I'm a decent Christian woman. The people in the church will talk about me.

NOVELETTE
Church people talking about others how ungodly?

PATSY
Novelette! Please. Could you just give me the same thing like every week. A nice wash and set. A simple uptwist, with three hairpins thanks. 'Cause that will not suit me.

NOVELETTE
Alright. But you know what Patsy, you cannot continue too resist change so it makes no sense worrying about it.

> *NOVELETTE touches PATSY's hair. As her fingers root themselves deeply into PATSY's hair, the GRI-OTS sing a peaceful melody and PATSY walks into her light. A preacher's voice is heard in the distance.*

PATSY (PREACHER)
And the Lord says who shall believe in me will receive salvation.

> *The spotlight settles on PATSY who walks down to the edge of the stage.*

PATSY
Romey use to say "Mom you worry too much. Ain't nothing ever gonna happen to me. "And then he would smile that easy slow smile that crept across his beauti-ful face. And those eyes, eyes full of mischief. Eyes that always let me know that child was up to something. (*beat*) Like taking four cookies instead of two. Changing that C minus on his report card to some messed up looking A, or sneaking in here at two a.m. when he knew his behind was supposed to be home by twelve-thirty. That child had me fooled for awhile, turning back all the clocks in the house, and me not even knowing he was late! Until I turned up at church Sunday morning and found out that

I had missed an entire hour and a half of Sunday Service. And Pastor Thomas not looking too impress with me, rolling in late for church. Sister Rosemary huffing and a puffing because I had missed my choir solo and Sister April had to sing it. And everybody knows that woman is stone deaf. Only reason she's in the choir because she and Pastor Thomas got a little something going on. Oh the flesh is weak child! And that boy making me miss my solo, was I ever mad. I tell you that day I prayed to the Lord to give me strength to deal with that boy. And when I got home, some divine intervention got into me and I cut up his behind. (*sings to herself*) God bless the child. (*laughs to herself*) Six-three, real tall you know, but I still wasn't afraid to give him something. (*beat*) But nothing could stop Romey. Oh with that boy there was never a dull moment. But he was a good kid. Yes he was. (*beat*) I would say Jerome. I would call him Jerome when I get serious or I got something important to say. Otherwise he was just Romey, my Romey. And I remember that night, I said, Jerome I don't have a good feeling about this. Why don't you and Damion rent some movies and I'll fix you some Kool-aid, order some pizza and you boys just can stay in. The streets are not safe for young boys. (*beat*) And Romey rolled his eyes and smiled that easy slow smile and kissed me right here. (*points to the area on her forehead*) Right here on my forehead. And he said "Mom, you worry too much, nothing going to happen to me. And besides Mom, we ain't on the streets it's a school dance. Nothing going to happen at a school dance. And Mom you know Denna Stewart going to be there, and you know I got a thing for Denna Stewart. I'm gonna show her my moves on the dance hall and she's gonna be all mine." (*She laughs.*) Po' Denna Stewart having that boy step all over her feet. And we laughed. Romey's he got this real deep happy laugh. (*beat*) But I guess everybody is happy when they laugh right? And before I know it Damion's at the door, honking the horn. And Romey's racing down the front step. And I said (*very urgent*) "Jerome! Be careful." And he smiled that easy slow smile. And he said "I'll be home by twelve-thirty" and I said "you better be in here by twelve a.m." and he took off running. And we both knew he wouldn't be home till twelve-forty-five. That's Romey always trying to get away with something. But he was a good kid. My boy was good. And that's all I said "be home by twelve." And

he was gone. (*beat, emotion begins to build, voice wavers*)
And I'm real mad with myself. Cause I thought I should
have told him wear your brown coat cause it's a real
warm coat. But I let him leave wearing the blue one and
that not a real warm coat. And I should have told him I
loved him—(*yells out*) I love you! And I should have just
listened to that rotting feeling in my gut and begged him
to stay. (*yells out*) Stay home Romey! But I didn't. I should
have just said (*yells*) Wear your brown coat Romey, it's
a warmer coat! Because he was lying on the ground you
know, on the cold hard ground. Bleeding to death. And
maybe if he was just wearing his brown coat—maybe the
coat would have kept him—maybe... But brown coats
don't protect little black boys from eights bullets do they.
Cause Damion said they were outside in the school parking lot. Romey was talking to Denna. And one minute he
was laughing, and there was a bang and Romey fell to the
ground. And by the time the police came the only people
left in the parking lot was Damion and Mr. Roland. He's
Romey's—he was, Romey's history teacher. He took his
jacket off and put it on Romey to keep him warm. At the
funeral I thanked him for that, you know for trying to
keep my baby warm. (*two beats*) No one knows who did
it. No one knows why? And no one is talking about it.
There was no witnesses. No witnesses? Nearly two hundred kids in a parking lot and no one saw anything. But
someone shot Romey three times. Three times and my
baby's gone. Because they killed him! They can do that!
Your son can kill my son just because! Because, maybe he
didn't like the colour of his jacket, or maybe he felt some
sort of disrespect because someone stepped on his shoe
in a club, But they are killing each others! (*two beats*) And
the police claim they are doing all that they can. But who
is protecting our children from some of them police. How
much is my son's life worth? (*beat*) Why do you need a
license to shoot a damn bird! You go to jail for leaving
your dog outside! But my baby, can lie on the ground for
twenty minutes before someone calls an ambulance. (*beat*)
Because there is no sign posted "warning Black boys are
in danger of becoming extinct." How come they can't
grow up to be Black men? (*three beats*) And I know as a
mother, you're suppose to love them, teach them, keep
their butts in line, tell them to wear brown coats instead
of blue—but you're not suppose to bury them! (*beat*) A
mother isn't supposed to bury her son... (*three beats*) I

took my ultrasound yesterday. And it's a boy. Me a mother again? And I thought about you Romey. Maybe he'll have your slow moving easy smile. Or maybe he'll have your eyes. Eyes full of mischief. And I cried. Cried for my baby. Right there in the waiting room I bawled, nose running and everything, a real ugly kinna cry. I cried for my sons. Cried for our sons. (*two beats*) And all the other mothers in the waiting room, they just looked away. Just looked away. Cause they understood. (*beat*) No, they understand.

> *The "waiting room" mothers who have been sitting frozen in tableau start a funeral procession. They throw dirt and state the names of several men. These are the names of young Black men who have been murdered. After the last name. PATSY joins them, and states Jerome Davis. PATSY returns back to the chair and the lights change. NOVELETTE's hands are still in her hair.*

NOVELETTE
So there you go a nice wash and set. This hair is growing, nice and thick. You know, they say a woman's hair grows when she's pregnant.

PATSY
Miss Novelette, what are you saying to me?

NOVELETTE
You a breed right? There's a bun in the oven!

PATSY
Letty, how did you know? I haven't told anyone but my husband and God.

NOVELETTE
I know.

PATSY
Oh, Letty, I don't know if I can do this again. You know with Romey and everything... and what if I'm not a good mother and maybe it's too soon. And and— I just can't help thinking about Romey and if I had only... (*sighs*) and maybe I'm too old. Novelette you think I'm too old?

NOVELETTE

Patsy, can you put your foot on your husband shoulder?
Come on Patsy talk to me! Pasty, can you put your ankle
around his neck and let him kiss it? Patsy, I know you
can do it. Because if you can do all of that, Patsy, you're
not too old! And I'm no Christian or anything, but I
believe God knew you had a lot more love to give so he
decided to give you another chance. I knew Romey and
that boy was a good kid. Well mannered, well-spoken
beautiful young man. And who could forget that smile.
And good kids don't raise themselves Patsy. So you were
a good mother. And you know now your going to be the
best baby mother around. You know there is a reggae
song, called, (*singing*) Claudette give me a beat 'you are
de best best best, baby mother'.

> *NOVELETTE starts to do a little reggae dance,
> EVERYONE joins in doing the latest dance moves.
> PATSY stiffly shakes to the beat.*

CLAUDETTE

Patsy you know dis is the latest dance move! Yes
Novelette you get it! Yes Patsy you are di best baby
mudda!

PATSY

Enough! Claudette, I'm a married woman I'm not trying
to be nobody's baby's momma.

NOVELETTE

No but you're going to be the best.

> *She attempts to pay NOVELETTE, but NOVELETTE
> waves her away.*

NOVELETTE

But don't be telling everybody because you know how
dem stay already.

> *PATSY laughs and heads towards the shop door.*

PATSY

Can I look for you in church on Sunday?

NOVELETTE
Look very hard!

PATSY
I'm going to pray for you child.

PATSY exits stage.

NOVELETTE
Ok, lunchtime! Claudette run next door to Maxine, and see if she has any of that fly fish ready and get me steamed rice with it.

She takes the money out of her bosom and pays her.

DIANA
Get me a piece of bread pudding and a soup and tell her to put some dumpling in it this time. How can a woman make soup with no dumpling? That's a lazy woman. Tell her to put it on my tab.

MARCIA
Claudette, a beef patty please.

She hands her some money and CLAUDETTE proceeds to leave.

NOVELETTE
And don't spend all day over there chatting with Maxine. Come, Marcia, I ready for you.

ENID comes rushing in as MARCIA is seated in the chair.

ENID
Miss Novelette, I'm going to need your magic!

NOVELETTE
Miss Enid! Is that you! My God I haven't seen you in ages. The last time I seen you was at...

ENID
Aston's funeral. It's been that long. I've been staying at my daughter's place for awhile. You know it was hard being in the house all alone so I was just helping her out with the kids.

NOVELETTE
Nice. How's your grandchildren doing?

ENID
Big. You know how they grow up overnight. Would you believe, Little Liddia is already wearing a training bra?

NOVELETTE
Little Liddy! Little Liddy got bitty titties!

ENID
Girl, she has a bra, make-up, cell phone and everything! How's your Renee doing?

NOVELETTE
Away in university. Just got me a call from her last night. "Mommy, send me some money, I need to buy a biology book." Well as long as she's studying the biology in the book and not with no boy! Dese kids nowadays! But I miss her, the house is so quiet.

ENID
I know...

NOVELETTE
But really how you doing?

ENID
Novelette I'm good real good. But you ain't going to believe this but—

NOVELETTE
Miss Enid don't say another word, get in my chair!

> *NOVELETTE and Miss ENID rush towards the chair. NOVELETTE attempts to push MARCIA out of the chair.*

Marcia get up, Miss Enid is here!

MARCIA
Hey but I was next!

SHARMAINE
I'm sorry Miss Enid, but I—

NOVELETTE
Respect your elders! And learn the value of patience.

SHARMAINE
But—

DIANA
Lord, Sharmaine. It's much more graceful to act as a lady
than a common street fighter, fighting over a hairdressing
chair! Lord, that is so common.

> *MARCIA grudgingly gets out of the chair. Miss
> ENID wastes no time and jumps in. At that exact
> moment SHERELLE rushes in, with her briefcase and
> phone in her hand.*

SHERELLE
Novelette, I need to be in your chair and out of here in
an hour! I got a lunch date at twelve and I got dinner at
six and I'm meeting my sister at nine and some where in
between all that I got to take a power nap. So let's do this!

NOVELETTE
Well. Let me tell you something Sherelle. I have just put
Miss Enid in the chair, and I still have to finish off Milly.
And there's at least two more women before you. And
Miss Brown just called and said she is sending her bad
pickney over here any minute now and I still need to eat
my lunch. And somewhere in between all of that Sherelle,
I need to take a power nap.

SHERELLE
Novelette! Could you not just squeeze me in please!

NOVELETTE
Next week. I'll put you down for my first appointment.

SHERELLE
(*looking disappointed*) Next week! But Novelette my roots
are growing in and I can't go in on Monday looking like
this!

NOVELETTE
(*not looking up at her as she starts to prep Miss ENID's hair*)
Well if you want to wait, maybe I can squeeze you in at
the end but not now I'm busy.

SHERELLE
But Novelette, I can't wait I—

NOVELETTE
Sherelle, don't wait then! I'll see you next week, be here for seven am.

SHERELLE
Novelette but I—

NOVELETTE
Listen, Sherelle just because you have some big fancy job and some big fancy education that doesn't mean you can come in here and tell me how to run my shop. I'm a career woman too. I know I couldn't walk into your fancy office downtown without an appointment and demand Sherelle, see me now! No you would run me! Now I tired of you now! I'll see you next week. Next week Sherelle! Next week!

> *A dejected SHERELLE exits the salon as the other women whisper who does she think she is... Lights fade on Salon and follow SHERELLE into her apartment. The phone rings and she answers it.*

SHERELLE
Hello? Hey Angie no—don't worry Angie, I can lend you the money. No don't worry about paying me back it's ok. Well I couldn't stand by and watch you lose your house. Ok. I'll deposit the money in your account tomorrow. Yep I'm fine, just tired. Umm kiss the boys for me make sure. (*She hangs up phone, and it rings again.*) Hey Donna I wanted to talk to you about—Oh Davey's in the hospital again. Don't worry that kid is a trooper. Give him some Wheaties and a plate of Mom's cornmeal dumplings and that kid will be fine. (*pause*) Well when you have some time we can get together. Hang on the other line, ok I'll let you go. (*She answers the other line.*) Hello? Yes Mr. Walters I closed the deal. I'll have the report on your desk Monday morning. (*pause*) No it's not a problem, I'll come in. You'll have it on your desk by noon tomorrow. You have a goodnight sir. (*She hangs up phone looking defeated.*) Bastard! Oh do I mind working on a Sunday. Well if you have just worked seventy-four hours for the week hey what's another ten! (*She sighs.*) Try walking into a room full of stuffy old white men in outdated expensive suits. You know, the old boys network, and try explain to them, MNAs, derivatives, calls, stocks and bonds— and then comes the looks and the unspoken questions

and the polite question. "Where did you study?" Just
checking to make sure the Black girl's got a high school
diploma. Then when I tell them I got a PhD in economics
from Yale, either it shuts them the fuck up or gets them
hard. All of a sudden I'm not the hired help, but a good
exotic lay. And naturally I'm supposed to jump at the
chance, because of course I've slept my way to the top.
Or I am the lucky recipient of affirmative action, employ-
ment equity or some old White man's guilt. A little old
man who maybe thought he needed some colour in his
office when getting his morning coffee. But not too much
colour. Don't be acting too Black because then they have
to deal with my blackness every day. So I put my blackness or lack of blackness in some women of colour box
to make you more comfortable. I'm tired of dealing with
them and them not wanting to see me! Trying to always
prove myself. Pulling sixteen hours days, skipping lunch-
es, not knowing it was actually ok for me to leave the
office and go home. Because I had to prove to them that I
could do this! I could do this! I could do my job! Sherelle
can do it! Of course Sherelle can! I can do everything!
(beat) And if not my job, it's Mom, Donna, and Angie.
You know the family shit! Everyone needs something
from Sherelle. Cause she's got it all. The great job. No
kids. Single by choice. The great house. The fancy car.
Everyone wants to be me, except me. So if your husband
leaves you call Sherelle, she'll know what to do. Your kid
is sick or skipping school call Sherelle, she'll know what
to do. You run out of money, call Sherelle! Mom, needs a
drive to No Frills, call Sherelle! You want a friggin report
on your desk Sunday not Monday, call Sherelle! I'm tired
of looking after everyone. Being the responsible one. The
good one. The one with all the answers, the level headed
one. (two beats) Mom calls me the glue. She says that I'm
the one who keeps this family together. (beat) So would
it be ok for me to just fall apart sometime? How would
you handle it if I told you that I get scared sometimes.
Lonely. Empty. If I was weak could you hold me up, glue
me together, patch me up, so I could deal with my shit
and your shit too! Cause I'm falling apart you know! I'm
disappearing. I can't believe I'm still walking. (beat) My
legs fell off three months ago you know? My arm just dis-
appeared last week. And yesterday I reached for my coffee and my fingers dropped off one by one and nobody
noticed. Nobody noticed I was gone. Just gone... And

today I spoke and I couldn't hear me! I couldn't hear my voice! I couldn't hear me! So you see I'm not really here you see and nobody noticed... (*two beats*) I was tired! I couldn't do this! I couldn't be everything! I couldn't—and it's not really that I wanted to die, I just wanted to take a rest. A long needed rest. But nobody would let me. They wouldn't let me! (*two beats*) I wouldn't let me...

> *She reaches for the pill bottle, and stuffs the pills into her mouth and swallows the water. She stares, eyes wide open at the audience. She slumps to the ground. The GRIOTS enter and surround her. They start in hush tones in synchrony. "But she had everything." "She was so beautiful." "Why?" "She had a really nice car." "She had everything." The last GRIOT hums a heartbeat melody. Lights go down on SHERELLE, and raises up on NOVELETTE and ENID in shop. BLOSSOM walks in.*

BLOSSOM

Hey Letty.

NOVELETTE

Blossom did you see Claudette out there? Where is that girl with my lunch, I am losing weight drastically by the minute!

> *MAXINE rushes in.*

MAXINE

Claudette, said to tell you she'll be back... next week something came up.

NOVELETTE

What!

MAXINE

(*shrugs her shoulders*) Hey don't shoot the messenger. Well, here's all your order, one flying fish, with rice and peas.

NOVELETTE

I wanted steam rice.

MAXINE

No steam rice today it finish. Maybe tomorrow. And here's your veggie patty.

MARCIA

I wanted beef.

MAXINE

No beef today maybe tomorrow or next week and the soup for?

DIANA

Let me guess, no dumpling.

MAXINE

Yeah sorry about that, guess it your unlucky day.

DIANA

Unlucky day? What does luck have to do with my food! Are you running a restaurant or The Niagara Casino? One day you maybe lucky one day you're not! How can you have soup without dumpling! And what about my bread pudding?

MAXINE

Well... maybe tomorrow—go ask the cook it's not my fault!

DIANA

You want me to go over there and ask about my dumpling! If I go over there you see!—

MAXINE quickly rushes out the door. NOVELETTE blocks DIANA from chasing after her in a mad frenzy.

NOVELETTE

Diana it's much more lady like to gracefully accept disappointment than fighting like a common street fighter over a dumpling! that's so common!

Everyone starts to laugh including DIANA.

ENID

Miss Diana don't raise your blood pressure. Cause today is your lucky day! You know I just baked me a sweet potato pie this morning and I can get my daughter to run it over. There's surely enough for everybody and if not I'll make some more! You know how I love to bake. And Charlie oh, he just loves my sweet potato pie—

NOVELETTE

Charlie? Who's Charlie?

ENID

Well... let me tell you girls... I got me a date tonight. Who would've thought there's any more oil in this ol' engine? But I revved it up and I'm rearing to go. And don't be thinking I'm some old little hussy, thinking I'm Demi Moore and getting me some young play thing. Oh no! I didn't go to a bar and throw my head back and bat my eyes and complain about the music being too loud as I picked up some boy young enough to deliver my morning paper! No I didn't. I just hopped the fence and found me somebody. (*She blushes.*) Well I didn't really hop the fence, you know Charlie, he lives next door. Ladies, I'm here to tell you, you ain't never too old to find love. And I got me a man. A good man. Let me tell you.

Two beats.

I had baked a nice sweet potato pie and my daughter was supposed to come over with the grandkids and then she called and said her youngest had swallowed a penny. I tell you, I think that child is going to be mean like his daddy! Oh his daddy is a stingy brute. Rather than pay for a real wedding, he eloped. Took my daughter down to city hall, that is so classless. City hall! It almost broke my heart. Every time I think about it, my blood pressure goes up. No church wedding. No reception. Just because he's cheap. A cheap, mean brute! So as I was saying, my grandson had swallowed a penny. I tell you there's the proof, that kid cheap like his daddy. Rather swallow a penny than spend it. (*shakes her head*) So Odette, that's my daughter, had to take that penny swallowing cheap idiot to the hospital. And that left me stuck with an entire sweet potato pie all for myself. And really I could've eaten it myself. Because ladies, there comes a time in your life where you ain't got no time to be watching your figure or worrying about your thighs and your butt. You just glad that the good lord has blessed you with another day and you still remember where your butt supposed to be. 'Cause when you get to my age, the memory sure

does fail you. Can I get a witness? Amen. Yesterday I put
my eyeglasses in the fridgerator, and the eggs in the med-
icine cabinet. Oh lord! (*She laughs.*) Bless this old girl. So
where was I? I told you about this memory. Oh the pie.
So I had me my pie. Standing in the kitchen just me and
my pie. And I looked outside my kitchen window and
there was Charlie pruning his tomatoes. The sun beating
down on him. Charlie was looking hot! I'm talking about
the sweating kina hot, dirty birdie! But yeah Charlie was
hot, I must admit, real hot! And then I felt this sort of tin-
gling feeling in my stomach and the tingle spread to some
other places I'm too much of a lady to mention. And I
thought, I hadn't had this sort of feeling in so long... it's
been so long. Lord, I can't even remember how long. (*two
beats*) Aston been dead seven years now. And even when
we were married, I never got me that tingly feeling like
the one I had for Charlie. Five kids. A mortgage to pay.
Breakfast, lunch and dinner to make. Somehow you forget about that tingly feeling and it becomes a dull ache,
a low moan and then all of a sudden it's just gone. Gone
just like that... And the only thing left to discuss is what
time "Wheel of Fortune" is starting. And it's not that I
didn't love Aston. Oh I did. It's just in my day you didn't
really marry for love or tingly feelings. You married a
good man. A man who would take care of you. A man
who would put his pay cheque on the table every Friday
night and put his shoes under your bed. And wake up
and go to church on Sunday. A man who you didn't have
to worry about that he was drinking away your mortgage
or had some young little floozy calling your house. No,
Aston was a good man. I miss him. I do... He took me to
Niagara Falls for our thirtieth anniversary. That's where
we first met on the State side 'cause that's where me and
my people are from. It was nice. I do miss him. (*sighs*)
Aston gave me five beautiful kids. Gave me peace of
mind... Gave me a nice home. But he never gave me that
tingly feeling like Charlie. But I loved him. Still do. He
was my best friend. (*shakes her head*) God bless him. (*two
beats*) So where was I? Girl, it's the memory! Oh yeah, in
the kitchen. So there I was feeling all tingly in my kitchen,
wanting to wipe that sweat off Charlie's brow, thinking
all kind of indecent thoughts. (*getting into a sexual heat*)
Thinking I would like to get me some Charlie, oh what I
would do with Charlie! I would put him on my kitchen
table and I—(*She catches herself.*) Well before I knew it, I

couldn't help myself I was marching out the back door and I leaned over the fence. Batting my eyes, throwing my head back. And I said, (*seductively*) "Mr. Charlie (*beat*) would you like some of my pie?" (*two beats*) And Charlie looking all sweaty and hot, real hot, said, "I sure would like a slice Miss Enid. Is it still hot?" And I said, (*seductively*) "it's real hot Mr. Charlie, but I'm sure it can cool down." And before I knew it Charlie hopped the fence, oh yes he did just hop over that big tall fence and there we were on the kitchen table. I mean around the table. Me and that fence hopping man. (*beat*) Ok, I'm exaggerating, but hopping the fence just sounded so much more romantic. But the man seventy-eight years old. He's got arthritis. He can barely make it up the stairs much less hop the fence. But there he was in my kitchen (*beat*) And we talked for hours. I poured him a long glass of ice tea. And we sat in that kitchen talking and laughing. (*She laughs real laugh.*) Ate the whole pie by ourselves. And Charlie leaned over and said, "Miss Enid, I do love me a woman, a big woman who ain't afraid to eat or laugh too loud." And I just put my head back, batted my eyes, patted my stomach and laughed real loud. And I said, "Mr. Charlie. (*very slow*) I do love me a man who knows how to eat some good pie."

She laughs really loud to herself.

Lights fade.

trey anthony   *photo provided courtesy of John Karastamatis*

l to r, front: d'bi.young, trey anthony, Satori Shakoor, Ngozi Paul, Jully Black
back: Quancetia Hamilton   photo provided courtesy of John Karastamatis

Ngozi Paul   photo provided courtesy of John Karastamatis

l to r: Rachael-Lea Rickards, Ngozi Paul, Raven Dauda, trey anthony, Abena Malika, d'bi. young, Miranda Edwards   *photo provided courtesy of John Karastamatis*

l to r: Ngozi Paul, Raven Dauda, d'bi.young, Abena Malika, Miranda Edwards, Lisa Codrington, Ordena Stephens-Thompson

photo provided courtesy of John Karastamatis

Act Two

Bathroom Scene

The women on stage except for NOVELETTE.

The women in the bathroom doing something to their hair while looking in the mirror. Soundscape of daily hair noises.

LADY ONE

So the brotha said he would call on Tuesday. It's now Saturday and there's no call. But it was our third date and I gave it up. You think that was too soon? But boy when he whispered to me, baby, I like the way you smell. Baby, the way you feel baby, I even like your toes and baby, your nose. I was in heaven. And then he grabbed my hair and pulled it ever so softly and said "baby, I like your hair."

LADY TWO

The naps are showing, I'm perming this.

LADY THREE

What the hell is this on my face! Oh no not a zit I got a date tonight! I'm cancelling!

A brother once said to me, "baby, I wouldn't usually give you the time of day, but you're kinna pretty for a dark skin girl." Pretty for a dark skin girl! (*two beats*) What am I going to do with this hair?

LADY FOUR

I want to be bald, sexy and bold. I think women are sexy when they are bald. Bald. Sexy and Bold. I'm thinking about shaving my head? I need a break. This shit is getting tired. I think I want to go for the natural bald sexy and bold look.

LADY FIVE

I was once bald. Oh yeah. I told the hairdresser, (*An image in silhouette. A woman tapping her feet. Two women reenact the following scene :*) "Excuse me. I think you keeping the perm in too long. My head's burning." She said...

LADY SIX
> Do you want it to be straight or what? A couple more minutes!

LADY FIVE
> So I just sat there. Clock ticking.

ALL THE WOMAN
> Tick tock. Tick tock. Tick.

LADY FIVE
> Clock ticking. Thinking about all the things I'm going do with my straight hair. Feeling my hair burn. Clock ticking.

ALL THE WOMAN
> Tick tock. Tick tock. Tick.

LADY FIVE
> I just sat there. Feeling my hair burn. Clock ticking. Hair burning. Bit my lip. Clock ticking.

ALL THE WOMAN
> (*faster*) Tick, tock, tick.

LADY FIVE
> Forty-five minutes later all my hair was falling down the sink. I had one tuff of hair left just here on the top. One piece. But boy was it straight!

LADY SIX
> Well all my sisters have curly hair. Curly like my Mom. I wanted curly hair. So what's a sister to do?

ALL TOGETHER
> Get a Jheri Curl!

LADY SIX
> You ever wash a Jheri Curl and all you had left was a Jheri and no Curl. And remember how you had to sleep with that plastic bag on your head. Your man wants to get romantic with you and you have a plastic bag on your head, because you don't want to grease up the sheets. Jheri Curl juice always dripping on your clothes, getting in your eye.

LADY TWO

> I had my hair braided so tight that my eyes hurt. And can
> I tell you about the itch, I had to pat it.

> *All the women start patting their heads.*

ALL TOGETHER Don't itch it, pat it!

LADY TWO

> I wonder if Bo Derek had to pat her head. Being that she
> was the first woman to ever wear braids.

LADY THREE

> You ever kept your braids in so long that when you took
> them out they were dreads?

LADY FOUR

> That's happened to me!

LADY ONE

> Me too! Three times! Maybe I should just lock my hair
> so then I wouldn't have to spend four hours taking the
> braids out and ten more hours to put them back in.

LADY TWO

> I'm going to lock my hair. Beautiful long locks. (*two beats*)
> My mother would kill me! (*two beats*)

LADY FIVE

> You ever had your hair hot comb and got caught in the
> rain. I remember I was terrified of getting my hair wet.
> I would watch the news every morning and if there was
> any sort of rain storm I wasn't leaving my house. A light
> drizzle, summer shower, thunder storm. I ain't going.

LADY TWO

> That's why Black women can't swim because we're
> scared about getting our hair wet. I remember my mom
> would say.

ALL TOGETHER

> Don't get your hair wet! you think you're White?

> *Bathroom scene ends.*

*Fade to black and lights up in salon. NOVELETTE
speaks to SHARMAINE.*

SHARMAINE

(*seated in the chair*) Wow! Miss Enid looked great!

NOVELETTE

Love looks good on her. And her hair has never looked
better!

SHARMAINE

Novelette you're magic. You know you're one of the
best hairdressers that I know and I've had some of the
so-called best work on me.

SHARMAINE

You're the best! Letty why don't you come to Hollywood
with me and you could be my personal hairdresser. The
weather's nice, I got a guest house you could stay there
rent free. I could pay you—

NOVELETTE

No, No Sharmaine. I'm happy right here. More than
happy with what I got. It's enough.

SHARMAINE

Your right but it was worth a try. Just feeling a little
homesick you know. But Letty I was thinking maybe I
should get an auburn something bright, or red bright
streaks! Or maybe I should go back to my natural colour?

NOVELETTE

Well if you can remember what your natural colour was
please let me know!

SHARMAINE

Ok red it is and—

MARCIA

So, Sharmaine, I am still waiting on the info about your
new guy...

SHARMAINE

(*sighs*) Marcia, there's no new guy.

NOVELETTE

I don't understand you, you know Sharmaine. Always
doing your hair, doing your nails. Such a pretty woman
and you don't have nobody. Career, career. And it's
important for a woman to have a career. But a career
won't hold you at night. You mean to tell me Sharmaine,
you can't find a decent man! You know what your problem is? You are too picky but I am going to help you out.
(*SHARMAINE looks up at her in distress ,everyone knows
what a disaster NOVELETTE's hook ups have been.*) Nope
don't say a word Sharmaine. I'm going to help you out.
I have a nice friend called Bunny who is quite nice. A
handsome guy. Tall dark and handsome. Six two and
strapping a decent job. Nothing is wrong with Bunny.
Nothing at all. Well… (*pauses*) The only thing which
might be wrong with Bunny is… he has two teeth miss-
ing at the front—

*All of the other women in the salon burst out laugh-
ing.*

SHARMAINE

You got to be joking! Novelette I—

NOVELETTE

I told you, you were picky. That's nothing a good dental plan couldn't fix. You have a dental plan at your job
Sharmaine, maybe you could help poor Bunny out?

SHARMAINE

You're not serious!

NOVELETTE

Well you want a good man you help him out!

SHARMAINE

I think I'll be ok…

*NOVELETTE places her finger in SHARMAINE's
hair while mumbling.*

NOVELETTE

Every good woman needs a good man ain't nothing wrong with Bunny and his teeth. Showing off
because you are some big movie star now! Hollywood,
Hollywood!

The lights go down the GRIOTS sing an upbeat jazzy show tune as SHARMAINE steps into her spotlight.

SHARMAINE
I think the only thing I ever really knew I wanted to do was to be an actor. (*She smiles to herself and becomes very excited.*) I wanted to be an actor! I wanted to be a star! And I must have been around eight years old when I saw Lily Tomlin on TV and I knew then without a doubt that was what I was going to do. And my Mom she jumped right in! She was a believer from the start. Mom was always giving me her famous pep talks. Sharmaine you can be anything or do anything. You know sometimes if you want something Sharmaine, and you believe in something you just have to fight for it. No matter what other people tell you. Fight for what you want. (*two beats*) And I remember in grade three, Sarah Thompson got picked to be the main character for our class play. She got to be the sun. And to make matters even worse, Claire Wilkens got picked to be the moon. Miss Collins thinking she was being multicultural and adding a little Caribbean flavor to the whole production, did me a huge favor by casting me as the star. The star. The lousy star who was on stage for about two seconds and said one lousy line. (*very melodramatic*) "I am the star. I shine bright." Yeah the star sucked! And I went home and I was devastated. To me at eight years old the Hollywood dream was already over. (*She imitates her mom with a slight Caribbean accent.*) Come on Sharmaine; say I am the star I shine bright. (*She states it again a bit differently.*) I am the star I shine very bright. (*imitating her mom again*) You think they will notice if you put in one more extra word? (*beat*) It wasn't looking good. And then finally the night before the concert Mom figures it out. (*beat*) two a.m. and we're in the kitchen cutting out cardboard and gluing aluminum foil on to a huge cardboard cut out of a star. And picture this. The night of the concert. Sarah and Claire show up in their pretty little dresses and bows to read their ten million lines. Mom is sitting smack centre in the front row. (*Mom's voice, "Wait till you see my chile!"*) When the lights go down I watch from the sides of the curtain as mom grabs a flashlight out of her pocket and that's my cue to come out! Mom shines the flashlight on to the stage, I walk into my light. The light hits the aluminum foil nearly blinding the entire audience! The stage looks like it's on fire! I am in my

glory because all eyes are on me! Mom firm and steady
keeps shining the flashlight. Every one says, wow! and
then is silent as I say my one line. "I am the star, I shine
bright". Mom oblivious to the fact that some people were
nearly blinded, by my dramatic entrance. Jumps up and
yells Bravo! That is my chile she's going to be a star! She
claps the hardest and loudest. Tears of pride in her eyes,
as she graciously thanks everyone who tell her how cre-
ative and inventive she is and how my costume stole the
show. And we march over to Miss Collins, who is about
as equally pissed off as little Sarah and Claire. And Mom
said to her. "Miss Collins, I've always told Sharmaine,
there are no small parts just small actors. And of course
(*beat*) there are those with small minds that think little
Black girls shouldn't play the lead." (*She laughs.*) And that
was my mom always in the front row. Clapping the hardest and the loudest in my corner. Giving me the strength
and the courage to fight for what I wanted. And I needed
you. beat I still need you. (*two beats*) You wiping the tears
for every audition I didn't get. You told me I was beautiful when they told me I wasn't White enough, didn't act
Black enough, not short enough, too fat, and too skinny.
And every time I wanted to give up, you wouldn't let
me. You gave me the ammunition to keep going. Fight
for what you want Sharmaine. preparing me for battle.
But when I met Jasmine, my defenses were down. I fell
hard and fast. And I knew right then, that there were two
things I was supposed to do with my life. Be an actor
and love Jasmine. Me loving her, and she loving me. Two
women in love. Caught up with her, she was all up in
my head. I memorized her body, her taste, memorized
her like my favourite script. Not wanting to ever forget
her smile, her laugh, and how her touch makes me feel.
And I am in love. And no it's not easy. But I am learning
to deal with so call friends who turned their backs on me
once they found out. My girl not wanting to drink from
my pop anymore, because everybody knows what those
lesbians do right? But in the same breath she tells me how
she finally convinced her man to go down... town. (*laughs
bitterly, two beats*) And of course I always hear I couldn't
possibly be a lesbian because that's something only White
girls do, right? (*two beats*) And there's a certain kind of
pain that can permanently paralyse you when your own
sister tells you she doesn't want you around her kids
anymore because... just because. And I'm learning to deal

with the looks, the stares, people calling me sick. Making
our love sound like something unnatural and wrong. I am
learning to deal with their shit! And really I think I can
deal with them! Because you showed me how to fight! So
I can deal with shit! But I can't! Mom I—I can't deal with
your silence! I can't deal with the fact that you can't bear
to look at me anymore! I can't deal with the fact that my
name seems to get stuck in your throat. How you make
me feel that there really must be something really wrong
with me, if you can't love me anymore! (*beat*) And you
use to love me so desperately. I'm still the same person!
I'm still here! When did you stop being in my corner?
How could you let go of my hand now—When this is
the fight where I need you the most. And I miss you. I
really miss you. And I can fight. I have to fight. I can fight
for everything. I can fight everyone! (*two beats*) But you
didn't teach me how to fight you.

> *The GRIOTS sing a soft melody. SHARMAINE
> returns to the chair lights change. Lights come up with
> NOVELETTE's hands still in SHARMAINE's hair.
> SHARMAINE looks in the mirror.*

So what do you think?

NOVELETTE
I think, whatever, makes you happy makes you beautiful.

> *SHARMAINE looks up and realises that
> NOVELETTE "knows."*

SHARMAINE
Thank you.

NOVELETTE
You're welcome darling. (*two beats*) Ok, Miss Hollywood.
Pay up time. And you know something Sharmaine, you
need to be tipping me some big Hollywood money. Now
that you are some big Hollywood star. So no change. I
will just take this for my tip. Thank you.

SHARMAINE
You're welcome.

> *She walks over to DIANE's station and pays her.*

Thanks Diana.

> *SHARMAINE is about to leave the store but changes her mind. She stops in front of the store door and tries to get the attention of MARCIA who is now under the dryer.*

Hey Marcia! Marcia!

> *MARCIA comes out from under the dryer.*

Is it ok if I bring a guest to your party?

MARCIA
Of course, I'm dying to meet him!

SHARMAINE
Great, I'll let her know. You'll love her as much as I do.

> *She walks confidently through the door before MARCIA thinks this new information through.*

MARCIA
Her?

NOVELETTE
Her.

MARCIA
Her!

DIANA
Darling, even I have kissed a woman before myself when I used to live in Paris. It's a very chic and classy thing to do while in Europe.

MARCIA
She's a lesbian!

> *Blossom grabs her cell phone and immediately starts to dial anxious to share the juicy gossip.*

BLOSSOM
Girl, you'll never believe what I just heard…

> *STACEY-ANNE runs in giddy with excitement she steps on Blossom's foot. BLOSSOM cries out in pain.*

NOVELETTE
> Hey Hey, Miss Stacey-Anne. A bruk you want to bruk down mi shop! You don't see you step on Miss Blossom toe! You better apologise immediately right now!

STACEY-ANNE
> Sorry Miss Blossom.

NOVELETTE
> Stacey-Anne, this is a place of business, not a playground. And I'm not your mother you know, but I'm not afraid to beat anybody in my shop. As a matter of fact where is my belt?

STACEY-ANNE
> Miss Novelette! No! No! Sorry! Me never mean to bruk down your shop. And I have two juicy fruit gum leave and I save one just for you, so you can always have fresh breath miss Novelette.

NOVELETTE
> I beg your pardon little miss. An insult you want to insult me about my breath. (*beat*) Well thank you anyways. And I know you never mean to come in here and bruk down mi shop because if you bruk it down I will bruk you up. Anyway Give Miss Novelette a kiss, (*STACEY-ANNE leans in and kisses her.*) and how is your mother?

STACEY-ANNE
> Fine Miss Novelette. She's at work again. A Mr. Brown a look after we and him give me money to come do my hair. Miss Novelette you can perm my hair today please, please—because I want to have tall hair like my teacher at school.

NOVELETTE
> You want tall hair today Stacey-Anne.

STACEY-ANNE
> Yes please.

NOVELETTE
> Today? Well, Miss Novelette will see what she can do. But Stacey-Anne I know you are in Canada now and it's cold outside, but it is warm in here so you must can tek off, the jacket, scarf, and sweater.

STACEY-ANNE

(*She sits in chair.*) Me know Miss Novelette, but me still feel cold.

> *NOVELETTE places her fingers in STACEY-ANNE's hair. The GRIOTS starts to sing a soft melody. The lights go down and STACEY-ANNE steps into her spotlight.*

Mi excited mi come a foreign but lawd it cold! Mi love de feel a snow pun mi lip and mi luv to lick it off but lawd it cold! And no matter how much jacket, coat and sweater you wear it still cold! Mi wear three pair a long john, mi na know why dem call it long john because it catch mi right here. Mi wear three pair and mi still cold! (*points midway to her knee*) Bwoy Canada cold! But mi know sey mi lucky fi come a foreign because nuff people back a yard mad fi come a foreign. And when Granny hear sey Mommy did marry Mr. Brown him a mi stepfadda now. Granny sey you lucky you mudda marry Mr. Brown so now she can send for onnu. A Granny a she luv Mr. Brown. One time Mr. Brown send Granny two hundred Canadian dollar one time! When Granny get de money, she jump and dance, and grab up mi and Carrie. Dat a mi likkle sister and dance round de place. It was the funniest thing mi did ever see, every time mi think about it mi have to laugh. And Granny say Mr. Brown is the best ting which ever happen to dis ya family. And she tell mi nuff times, mi beg you Stacey-Anne when you go a foreign, do na do nothing which will make Mr.Brown mad cause him send fi onnu and him can send you right back! Mommy and Mr. Brown pick we up a the airport with Gary who is mi likkle bradda who mi never did see before. And Mommy cry and hug up mi and Carrie and she start bawl and say what a way you grow big. Lawd a six years now mi never see you. And Carrie grab up pun mi cause she never did remember Mommy. Cause she did one likkle baby when Mommy did leave and mi did six years old. But mi still remember Mommy. Mi remember she did wear one daisy smelling perfume, and when she hug mi a de airport mi did remember her. And Mommy did feel bad that Carrie na look like she remember her. And she ask Carrie if she did get di dress and di clip for we hair, and de socks and de soap powder,and de tin of bullybeef. And Carrie say yes but she still wouldn't go to Mommy, and she put down one piece of cow bawling for Granny, and she wouldn't let go a mi hand. And den now, Mr. Brown him did look like him a get mad. And him say to Mommy mi hope sey you no bring na spoil spoil pickney inna ei hope you no bringsey yu na badda bring na spoil spoil pickney inna mi house you know. And just try talk to dem inna de car because mi a park for parking. And him did look so vex mi did think him would a send we right back pun de plane we did come. So mi whisper to Carrie try no badda do nothing which will mek Mr. Brown mad. And Carrie musey stop bawl for one minute and sixty-two seconds and den she put down one next piece a cow bawling fi Granny.

But now Carrie git use to Mommy, but she still stick pun mi some time. And she na talk 'bout Granny much. And she luv her school, you know why, cause her teacher have yellow hair!, Mi mean blonde hair. And Carrie like her cause she remind her a woman pun Gilligan Island. You remember Gilligan Island? We use to walk must be two hundred twenty-two mile fi watch pink people with yellow hair pun TV, cause we never did have no TV a we yard. And mi like foreign now cause now mi have a TV inna mi room. And mi don't have to wear uniform go a school. And mi learn to talk properly and correctly. And mi have nuff nuff clothes, nuff nuff long john, and mi eat nuff nuff McDonalds and yam peanut butter sandwich every day with jam! And mi did tell you sey mi have mi own room? My own room. Cause in Jamaica mi and Carrie and Granny use to sleep pun one bed, in one room! But now in foreign mi have my own room. My own room for mi and mi alone!

She becomes quiet and looks down on the floor.

But sometimes Mr. Brown come inna a mi room. When Mommy gone a work a night time him come inna mi room. And him touch mi. And do things which Granny sey you should'nt mek bwoy do but Mr. Brown him do it. And first time mi did sey no Mr. Brown but him did look like him a go get mad. And remember mi did tell you, that Granny said mi shouldn't do nothing which will mek him mad. And mi no want him fi send we back, and mi no want him to stop send Granny de money. And Carrie she just a get use to Mommy and now she woulda really bawl if we have to go back now, cause Mr. Brown just buy her three new Barbie and him sey him a go buy we a dream house dolly house, big so! (*widens her arms to express the length*) And mi no want to go back now! And mi na want to mek him mad. So Mr. Brown happy when him touch mi and him want mi to touch him too... and when him inside mi it hurt... but mi don't say nothing to mek him mad. (*begins to beat her leg, mimicking the rhythm of sex*) So when him inside a mi, mi just think 'bout Carrie three new Barbie, Carrie teacher with her yellow hair, mi and Carrie laughing when we a eat McDonald french fries, and mi licking the snow offa mi lip. (*Two beats, and she hits her leg for the last time.*) And you know my favourite one to think about is Granny dancing with mi and Carrie when Mr. Brown send her the money. By the time Mr. Brown finish. (*beat*) Granny still a dance inna mi head...

> STACEY-ANNE *begins to hum and* GRANNY *enters dancing, very dreamlike, the other women enter and surround* STACEY-ANNE, *giving her energy and love. And they begin the song and dance of "healing." After the dance they all turn away with their back to the audience.* STACEY-ANNE *remains but she is no longer a little girl she is the voice of a grown woman she recites the following dub poem as the women keep the beat with their feet in a step dance.*
>
> "in honour of belief" by d'bi.young, a jamaican-born and raised dub poet who resides in Toronto Canada with her son, moon anitafrika.
>
> www.dbiyoung.net

in all parts of di world
live a little boy a little girl
who is crying a mommy for a daddy
for an auntie for an uncle for a granny
who is crying for a brotha a sistah a friend
to defend them from
di deep bitter bile

violating hands dat creep
beneath di sheet
when them a sleep
dis secret (secret)
a monster inna di closet

little girl little boy di moon is your witness
dis sickness
is no fault of yours
we carry the karmic shame
for not stepping in
and now you are to blame
little boy little girl di moon is your witness

little boy little girl di moon is your witness
dis sickness is no fault of yours
we carry di karmic scar
for not stepping in before it went too far
little girl little boy di moon is your witness

now di time has come
get off of di ground
no more a little girl a little boy
you are a womban you are a man
stand up strong

turn your face to the moon
and your spirit to the sun
and you SHINE without SHAME
this story is yours and mine to claim

little boy the moon is your witness
little girl the moon is your witness
little boy the moon is your witness
little girl the moon
the blue blue moon
is your witness
the moon is your witness
the moon is your witness

I believe. You said mumma it was poppa, but she never
did believe. Dem na believe. No body would believe sey
yu bradda hold u down, throw u pun de ground. Dem na
believe.

Mi know about da teacher who tell yu fi stay late a
school. Yes her teacher at school. Dem na believe.

And Uncle Henry who come to visit an could never find
him room. Every night him coming. Too often. Too soon.
Coming in mi room. Dem na believe. Dem na want to
believe.

It was your fadda, my step-father, Nicole's bradda, Linda's grandfather, Tamika's teacher at school, the neighbour, the priest, Uncle Henry, Uncle Dan, Marie's cousin, the man without a name. They left you. Fearful, rejected, abused and used. Taken things not given freely but nobody would believe. Dem na believe.

And if somebody just believed! You could become proud, strong, beautiful, please (*pause*) someone help her right the wrong. Sista, hold up your head, na badda hang it down. Look mi in my eye. Erase all doubt, sweep away the shame it wasn't your fault. I said it wasn't your fault… You just had to tell me once that it happen to you and I would tell you, Sista it happen to me too. And even it didn't and I was one of the lucky few, I would still believe you. I believe you. I believe. You believe me? All women all little girls should be believed. Do you believe? (*turns her back to the audience and then turns around abruptly*) Touch mi again you better run fi your life.

> *The women do an angry step dance and exit the stage.*
>
> *No one on stage except for NOVELETTE.*
>
> *NOVELETTE takes a seat in chair, removes her red wig and addresses audience.*

NOVELETTE
What did you think I was a natural red head! Well I got to get going 'cause I have a party to go to and ladies you know how long it takes for us to get ready. Nails, hair, outfit! And let's not forget all those little extras. But I cut out all those little extras. No more squeezing this body into a tight girdle. No I tell you. I'm loving this body now. Took awhile and a few hard lessons but now I'm loving every inch, every curve, every pound. It's all mine and I love it! Feed it good food, to keep it strong, healthy You have to nourish it. And mi go to gym, but I'm not killing or starving myself. And I don't know maybe it's age could be wisdom, or maybe it's working in this shop for so long. But I see far too many of you women rushing in here, trying to get it right. Be right. Do it right… and no matter what you do, you just don't feel right. Cause if you're not ok with the woman inside, nothing else matters. Nothing. (*two beats*) Anyway it's party time. I got to go! Party time these are the good times!

> *She gets up to leave, and NIA rushes in.*

NIA

Novelette I know I missed my appointment, but please could you just squeeze me in.

NOVELETTE

Listen here, Nia, I told you, come for four o'clock. It's now nearly nine o'clock.

NIA

Letty, you never start me on time.

NOVELETTE

That's not the point. An appointment to me isa guarantee that you will show up on time. An appointment doesn't mean that "A" I will start you on time or "B" you can come waltzing in here anytime you feel. Now the shop is closed. Day is finished. Shop lock up and time for everyone to go home and that includes you! Bye!

NIA

Please, Novelette, I got a funeral I'm going to tomorrow.

NOVELETTE

(*softening*) I'm sorry. I did hear about your mother, how are you doing?

NIA

Oh I'm doing ok, but I guess Sandy's taking it hard, her and Mom were close.

NOVELETTE

Well come Nia. What are you having?

> *She passes her the magazine but then quickly grabs it back.*

As a matter of fact you know something give me back my magazine. Because I have no time today for fancy hair styles, pictures in a magazine, and you wanting me to give you false hopes and promises, because I am a hairdresser—

NIA & NOVELETTE

Not a magician.

NOVELETTE

So what are you having?

NIA

As good as you are there are somethings that not even your magic can fix.

She looks in the mirror.

You know what take it off.

NOVELETTE

What? All of it? Are you sure?

NIA

Yes.

Lights transition and NIA walks into her spotlight.

Sandy held her breath, when you pulled back the blanket. Pity the bitch didn't pass out, while you were looking her baby over. I'll always remember how you smiled when you looked at his ears, then laughed out loud when you saw his even paler fingers. Sandy knew the shit was good, and she had passed again. (*beat*) I couldn't believe it. Couldn't believe the bitch was back on her pedestal. (*laughs bitterly to herself*) Yeah you knew she had skipped more classes than she had ever gone to. Hung out with the wrong crowd. Dropped out of high school because she was pregnant. But you conveniently forgot all of this because she had given birth to her light brown bundle of joy. (*two beats*) Her kid's hair was so wavy, I thought you would jump right in for a swim. You were such a proud grandmother. Quickly calling all the family and telling them how the baby could easily pass for White. (*shakes her head in disbelief*) And I just wanted to go over there and smack you in your damn Black ugly face, and ask you, what about me! What about Tasha? Did you know that Tasha's birthday was last week? Did you know that her kindergarten teacher said she's reading at a grade two level, and today she tied her shoelaces all by herself. But you wouldn't give a fuck would you because you can't find a wave in Tasha's hair. No good hair, no mistaking my baby for White. Her skin is black coffee, black coffee without the milk. And I know it's all my fault cause I chose to lay down with a man that if he closed his eyes and stopped smiling you would have thought he left the room. (*beat*) Midnight you called him, but personally I think he looks more like quarter past. And when Tasha was born you marched over to the hospital, hoping for the best but expecting the worst. And you got that didn't you? You didn't laugh when you looked at Tasha's dark fingers and even darker ears. And your face said it all. No need to speak Mom, because I had heard it all before. (*imitating her mother*) "How many times do I have to tell you girls pick the men you lay with because anything too black is never good." (*pause*) Anything too black is never good. Anything too black is never good! I should have known that because I was never good enough for you was I! You hated my blackness. Ranted and raved every Sunday afternoon as you heated up the pressing comb to press my bad hair. While Sandy ran outside. The good hair one. The light one. The right one. We stayed in the hot kitchen and I pinned my ears back holding my breath, not daring to move because I didn't want to get burnt again. And as you fried and cooked my bad hair, you cursed my blackness. Cursed my father. Hating, to see him in me, hating to see you in me, hating to see the black in me. (*two beats*) And you know I'm thirty-two years old and I still cry when I see little Black girls with red ribbons in their hair. You wouldn't buy me them you said I was too black to wear red. No little red dresses, or red socks. Cause I was too black for red. (*getting emotional*) Too black to wear red? And you know last week I bought Tasha fourteen red ribbons and put all of them in her hair, yep all fourteen of them in her hair. (*laughs to herself*) And Tasha looked in the mirror and laughed and said "Mommy, I think I got too many ribbons in my hair", and I said "no baby Mommy just like to see you in red. It's my favourite colour." (*two beats*) And I wanted to believe that you tried to love me, but I just couldn't feel it. I couldn't compete with Sandy. Because I lost that race before I even started. And I've been trying all my life to win it. Not to get you to love me as much as you love Sandy but just a little bit. And now you're dead. (*beat*) And I know I'm suppose to feel something. Maybe cry, maybe mourn. I want to feel something. And for God sake you're my mother and your dead! And I want to feel something and I can't. I want to cry and I can't. (*Two beats, she tries to convince herself.*) Maybe at the funeral I'll cry. Because I'm wearing a black dress, a black hat, black shoes, black stocking all black. All black. Mom, I'm wearing all black! Mom could you just look at me! I'm wearing all black! Please will you just look at me...? I'm wearing all black. (*three beats*) I've been wearing black all my life.

> *All the women enter individually and state proudly "I've been wearing black all my life." NIA looks at them. This sends them into a healing song, in which they rock together. They perform a healing ceremony which goes through various emotions of discovery, anger, self-healing and love. The dance also offers NIA pride, self-identity, comfort, love, and joy of being a black woman. The women dance a celebratory dance. This is a celebration. A celebration of life. They then close the coil from the opening scene. NOVELETTE enters the dance at the end... Inhales and exhales and smiles at them proudly and proudly states.*

NOVELETTE
I've been wearing black all my life.Blessings.

The End

"Working Session"

l to r: Ordena Stephens-Thompson, Raven Dauda, d'bi.young, Ngozi Paul, Miranda Edwards, Weyni Mengesha, Quancetia Hamilton

trey anthony – Playwright

"What I am trying to do is put Black culture on stage and demonstrate to the world—not to White folks not to Black folks, but to the world— that it exists and that it is capable of sustaining you. I want to show the world that there is no idea or concept in the human experience that cannot be examined through Black life and culture."

August Wilson.

trey anthony is the playwright of *'da Kink in my hair*. She is also the co-creator and co-producer of the television drama, "Kink in my hair," based loosely on the play which aired on Vision Television and is currently in development for a television series. Trey is a published playwright and her work has been seen in numerous publications. Trey is a former television producer for The Women's Television Network, WTN, and has written for the Comedy Network and CTV and worked on "The Chris Rock Show" HBO. She is also the Executive Producer of Canada's first Urban Womyn's Comedy Festival, 'dat girl sho is funny! The festival is an annual sold-out event and features women of colour comediennes. She is a 2002 Canadian Comedy nominee and in 2004 she was nominated for a Dora! She is busy working on her first screenplay, a hip hop love story and the sequel to *'da Kink in my hair*. In her spare time she enjoys pushing boundaries, questioning and redefining "the rules," creating safe spaces for womyn, and giving "Voice" to those not often heard.

"My hair roots me in my truth."

First edition: July 2005. Fifth printing: February 2019.
Printed and bound in Canada by Imprimerie Gauvin, Gatineau

Cover image: janet romero
Cover design: JLArt
Production Editor: MZK

**PLAYWRIGHTS
CANADA PRESS**
202-269 Richmond St. W.
Toronto, ON
M5V 1X1

416.703.0013
info@playwrightscanada.com
www.playwrightscanada.com
@playcanpress